Why Bully Me?

Written by
Cameron M. Fry
& Angel Bell

Illustrated by Dionna L. Hayden
Design/Layout by Pink Elephant Graphic Design
Published by D.I.R. 19 Publishing
Copyright © 2019 Cameron Fry | Copyright © Angel Bell

Paperback ISBN: 978-1-7346165-0-7   Hardcover ISBN: 978-1-7346165-1-4

dir19publishing.com | prodigythree.com | thinkpegd.com

Dedication

*For every boy and girl that has experienced
some form of bullying.
You are not what people say you are;
you are SMART, INTELLIGENT, and UNIQUE
—most of all you are a LEADER!*

"WHY BULLY ME?" is about a school age child who suffers from being bullied at school by another student and can't seem to understand why the bully decides to pick on him. As you continue to read, you will be able to identify some key facts about school bullies and types of bullying behavior:

☑ **Physical Bullying** – is bullying that takes the form of physical abuse, such as pushing, shoving, hitting, spitting, and tripping. Threats of physical harm and attempts to force people to act in ways they would prefer not to.

☑ **Emotional Bullying** – is bullying that involves factors other than physical interaction, such as insults, derogatory remarks, name calling, and teasing. Also includes ignoring the victim, which is referred to as social bullying. Emotional bullying could also take the form of purposely misplacing or hiding someone's belongings. Emotional bullying can be done in person or through cyber bullying.

☑ **Face To Face Bullying** – is bullying in which people confront each other in person.

SOURCES: wesleymission.org.au | stopbullyingnow.hrsa.gov | nces.ed.gov

Cameron is a friendly kid who always meets new friends. A lot of other kids have always attached themselves to him. He's like a magnet for being a great friend. Until one day in fourth grade there was this one particular kid that did not cling to Cameron or just did not quite find Cameron to be a cool friend.

His name is Richard. Richard was new to school, and would cause trouble with other students. He would disrupt the class by picking on other students or choosing to even destroy the class, by throwing objects around the classroom.

Well, it was Richard's second week of school, in Mrs. Kramer's fourth grade class, and the trouble begins, name calling, class disturbance, and disruptive behavior. During reading time Richard decided to pick on the student in front of him, Cameron. Cameron was always quiet, friendly, and very helpful, never caused trouble.

Richard thought that it would be a good idea to push Cameron. Mrs. Kramer caught Richard in the act and asked him, "Why did you do that to Cameron?" Richard did not give a response. Mrs. Kramer said, "Richard I need you to apologize to Cameron." Richard yelled, "NO! I do not like Cameron" (yelling with anger). So as the day went on, Mrs. Kramer still could not get Richard to apologize to Cameron for his behavior.

If Cameron got all of his homework right, Richard would say, "Yeah, I bet you cheated." So Cameron would hide his homework, by putting it in his other classmates' desks. If Cameron wore a new pair of shoes to school, Richard would say, "Your shoes are bigger than your body" (while there would be other students standing around laughing and pointing). If Cameron scored at basketball Richard would say, "You were just lucky." So Cameron decided to stop playing basketball.

Richard never asked Cameron to sit with him at lunch. Richard found a way to make room for all of his friends and Cameron sat alone. Cameron got tired of sitting alone so one day he got enough courage to try sitting at Richard's table. "Look at Bigfoot!" said Richard. Cameron's face burned with anger. He blinked to keep from crying. Cameron decided to just leave the cafeteria without finishing his lunch.

After school Cameron went directly to his room. He sat on his bedroom floor staring at the wall with worry, anger, and frustration. Wondering, *what will Richard have to say next?* At that moment, Cameron thought about Mrs. Kramer. She told the entire class that "Sometimes bullies stop bullying if you just ignore them." Cameron was still in deep thought, wondering *how you would ignore a bully who is always in your face.*

It was dinner time. As Cameron's mom prepared the dinner table, she asked, "How was school?" Cameron remained silent. Mom asked again, "How was school?" Cameron stopped and stared at his mom. "What's wrong?" asked mom. "Nothing," said Cameron.

That night Cameron couldn't fall asleep. He stayed awake thinking and wondering why Richard chooses to mess with him. Cameron fell asleep murmuring himself to sleep, saying, "Why bully me? Why bully me?"

The next morning, his eyes were heavy and his stomach was hurting. "Can I stay home today?" he asked his mom. His mom felt his forehead. "You don't feel no where near hot," "I have a stomach ache," said Cameron. "Hmmmm, I guess you are sick; you can go back to bed," said mom. Cameron finally fell back to sleep.

Cameron knew that he couldn't avoid Richard forever. So the next day, Cameron made his way back to school.

All morning Cameron ignored Richard. At gym time, he discovered that his mom had packed his gym clothes and he soon found out that the gym clothes his mom packed were not his, but his little brother Nathan's.

Cameron contemplated putting on the gym clothes because he knew that they would be too small, but he knew that if he did not get dressed he would risk receiving a bad grade. He left out of the locker room and walked into the gym with the too small shorts on, embarrassed and ashamed by what he had on. "Bigfoot has on his baby brothers shorts," Richard said to everyone. Cameron's fist started curling up and his eyes began to water with tears, he was just that angry and embarrassed. While thinking, *"how could my mom do something like that?"* he begins to walk away.

"Cameron, come sit over here," called Jacob. Cameron quickly sat down next to Jacob and his friends. "Richard is such a bully!" said Jacob. "You should really stand up to him." For some reason, Cameron couldn't.

When Cameron finally made it home he said to his mother, "You packed Nathan's gym clothes in my book bag. His clothes are too little for me." "Well Cameron, I was rushing out to get us all to our destinations this morning," said mom. "I do apologize." She paused. "What's the difference? You were still able to receive your gym points for class." "It makes a BIG DIFFERENCE," said Cameron. As he yells, storming up to his room.

"This just can't be about gym clothes," said mom. "It's about Richard," said Cameron, yelling with anger and frustration. "He picks on me. He calls me Bigfoot; today he teased me about Nathan's shorts." "Oh really?" said mom. "Have you let him know how you feel?" "No," said Cameron. "Then he would really make fun of me." "Why don't you talk to the principal Mr. Johnson?" Suggested mom. "If he knew that Richard was bullying you, he'd do something about it."

That night Cameron could not sleep. He tossed and turned, thinking if he should talk to Mr. Johnson? Should he try standing up to Richard? What could he say to him? *Your shoes are ugly. Your feet are the same size as my little brothers.*

The next morning Richard walked up behind Cameron in the hallway. "BIGFOOT!" Richard shouted. At that very moment Cameron's heart was pounding. He thought about what his mother said. He turned around and shouted out, "I'm going to tell Mr. Johnson, if you keep picking on me!" Cameron was face to face with Richard. "SNITCH," said Richard, and he stuck out his tongue as he flinched at Cameron, and then ran into the classroom.

At lunch, Cameron sat with Jacob again. Richard was at the table with his friends. "Hey, Bigfoot!" called Richard. "Did you wear your baby brother's gym shorts again?" Cameron stood up. He had enough of Richards's mouth. In a loud voice, he said, "I may have big feet, but I am confident in who God has created me to be! So WHY BULLY ME? I know who and whose I am! I'm a child of God!" Richard sat puzzled, lost and confused. For once, he did not say anything.

Cameron walked out of the cafeteria with his head held high, walking in confidence, as friends and other students stood around cheering and applauding Cameron, for standing up to Richard with confidence. Cameron made it home and his mother asked, "Did you stand up to that bully, Richard?" "Yes, I did, I don't think Richard will pick on me anymore," said Cameron. "But even if he does, I know what to do." "AWESOME Cameron!" said mom.

That night Cameron got on his knees, prayed and thanked God for giving him the right words to say to the bully, Richard. Cameron also prayed that God would touch Richard's heart so that, Richard can be confident in who God created him to be. Cameron then fell asleep confident and worry free!

Cameron M. Fry

Cameron Fry is 11 years old and in the sixth grade. Cameron's inspiration to write a book on bullying extended from an incident that he was involved in at school that consisted of him being in trouble along with other boys that he affiliated/socialized with who decided to bully/pick on another scholar in their class. At that time, Cameron and the other boys involved had to write a letter regarding the situation and present it to the bullied scholar and other classmates apologizing for their actions, because their actions could have caused the bullied scholar to take things into their own hands, hurting themselves or someone else. After Cameron's experience with that, and careful research on the causes and actions behind bullying, he was inspired to learn more and spread bullying awareness. Cameron looks forward to launching his "Why Bully Me?" awareness program which will be implemented in schools and several other organizations.

#TAGS: #DontSufferInSilence | #AntiBullying | #AntiBullyingAmbassador

Angel Bell

Angel Bell is the proud mother of one son, minister, author, mentor, life coach, consultant, and a visionary of purpose. She's currently working on completing several books, and working on the expansion of her consulting business, as well as other business ventures. Angel is the founder of Dreams Into Reality Coaching and Consulting Services, LLC (D.I.R.) and most of all, she is a Woman of God. She's an encourager and motivator by nature, she serves her community through a variety of ministries and community outreach programs at her church, Greater New Birth Church of Milwaukee, WI, under the great leadership of Bishop R. J. Burt and Pastor Patricia Burt. Angel is passionate about making a difference in the lives of others. She is a big advocate for helping people reach their full potential in all that they may set out to do, as well as to know that, with God, "ALL THINGS ARE POSSIBLE" (Matthew 19: 26). She simply believes that there is "no limit to whom or what you can be." God created you to be all that you can be, for his glory, divine purpose and will.

BOOKS *(Co Author)***:** Why Bully Me | Women of Courage (Volume II)
PROFESSIONAL MEMBERSHIP: The Professional Woman International Authors Bureau
CONTACT: Dreams Into Reality Coaching and Consulting Services, LLC
(414) 909-3174 | dreamsintorealityllc@gmail.com

Bullying and Cyber Bullying

- 45% of young people experience bullying before the age of 18.

- 36% of young people aged 8-22 are worried about being bullied at school, college or university.

- 38% believe their school; university or college doesn't take bullying seriously.

IMPACT OF
Bullying

- More than 16,000 young people are absent from school because of bullying.

- 83% of young people say bullying has a negative impact on their self-esteem.

- 30% of young people have attempted to commit suicide as a result of bullying.

- Those who have been bullied are more than twice as likely to have difficulty in keeping a job, or committing to something compared to those not involved in bullying.

- People who have been bullied are at great risk for health problems in adulthood, over six times more likely to be diagnosed with serious illness, smoke regularly, or develop a psychiatric disorder compared to people not involved in bullying.

(diana-award.org)

Bullying Display

1. Low self-esteem

2. Difficulty in trusting others

3. Lack of assertiveness

4. Aggression

5. Difficulty controlling anger

6. Isolation

SOURCES: wesleymission.org.au | stopbullyingnow.hrsa.gov | nces.ed.gov

CPSIA information can be obtained
at www.ICGtesting.com
Printed in the USA
BVHW021802260520
580356BV00010B/92